ARCHIMEDES RUSSELL

Upstate Architect

D1261861

A YORK STATE BOOK

Archimedes Russell

ARCHIMEDES RUSSELL

Upstate Architect

Text by
EVAMARIA HARDIN

Photographs by
JANE COURTNEY FRISSE

With contributions by
J. BRAD BENSON & MARY ANN SMITH

SYRACUSE UNIVERSITY PRESS
1980

Based on an exhibition organized by J. Brad Benson for the Institute for the Development
of Evolutive Architecture.

Preparation of this catalog and the exhibition at the Everson Museum of Art, Syracuse, New York,
was sponsored by IDEA, Inc., and was funded in part with public funds from the
New York State Council on the Arts.
Funding was also provided by Key Bank of Central New York.

Archimedes Russell, upstate architect.
(A York State book)
To accompany an exhibition on view Sept. 26, 1980–Jan.
11, 1981, at the Everson Museum of Art.
1. Russell, Archimedes, 1840–1915—Exhibitions.
I. Hardin, Evamaria. II. Frisse, Jane Courtney.
III. Benson, John Bradley. IV. Everson Museum of Art
of Syracuse and Onondaga County.
NA737.R87A4 1980   720'92'4   80-23601
ISBN 0-8156-0165-4 pbk.

Manufactured in the United States of America

CONTENTS

J. BRAD BENSON is currently Gallery Director for Associated Artists in Syracuse, New York. He holds a master of fine arts degree in museology from Syracuse University. He was responsible for organizing and curating an exhibition of the architecture of Archimedes Russell at the Everson Museum of Art (1980) in Syracuse, for which this publication served as a catalog.

JANE COURTNEY FRISSE is a free-lance photographer in Syracuse, New York. Her photographs have been published in a number of art and architecture publications, including *The Arts and Crafts Ideal: The Ward House* and *Cazenovia — The Story of an Upland Community.*

EVAMARIA HARDIN holds a master's degree from the Department of Fine Arts, Syracuse University, and specializes in nineteenth-century American architecture. She is a free-lance consultant for several central New York preservation organizations.

MARY ANN SMITH is Associate Professor of Architectural History in the School of Architecture at Syracuse University. She has published articles in various historical magazines and is an authority on the architecture of Gustav Stickley. Dr. Smith teaches courses in American architecture, documentation, and preservation.

PREFACE

Archimedes Russell was a nineteenth-century regional architect whose buildings have enhanced the landscape of central New York for more than a century.

Only a small portion of Russell's architectural legacy is presented here. The large number of commissions which issued from Russell's office was staggering, more than eight hundred over a fifty-year career; they included every kind of design, from porches to courthouses.

The following selection of Russell's most successful and best-known buildings illustrates ten of the styles in which he worked. The origins and chief characteristics of each style are first sketched, followed by more detailed discussions of Russell's buildings.

Some of the buildings, such as the H. S. White Chemical Engine House (plate 32, demolished long ago), are better known for their local historical associations than for their architectural merit. Others have served their inhabitants well for generations. Some have been unnecessarily destroyed. A selected list of major commissions which it has not been possible to illustrate follows the main text.

This book has been published so that it might accompany an exhibition which I organized in 1980, "Archimedes Russell: Architect of Syracuse." On view September 26, 1980–January 11, 1981, at the Everson Museum of

Art in Syracuse, New York, the exhibit was composed of original Russell drawings and photo murals. I would like to express my gratitude to the Institute for the Development of Evolutive Architecture (IDEA) for its sponsorship of the exhibit and this book. I would like to thank Cleota Reed and especially Donald Pulfer of IDEA for their assistance.

I selected the works to be illustrated and determined the arrangement of this book in the hope that it would not only complement the exhibition but would also stand alone as an independent volume on Russell. Credit for this publication is in good part due to the contributions of my associates. I would like to express my sincere admiration and thanks to Jane Courtney Frisse for her photographs, to Mary Ann Smith for her introduction, and to Evamaria Hardin for her text and captions.

Partial funding for the exhibition and this publication has been generously provided by the New York State Council on the Arts and by Key Bank of Central New York. Additional funds were donated by King & King Architects; Syracuse University; the Central New York Chapter of the American Institute of Architects; Sargent Webster Crenshaw & Folley, architects; and Joseph H. King, Jr. Assistance has been provided by the George Arents Research Library at Syracuse University, the Landmarks Association of Central New York, the Central New York Chapter of the American Institute of Architects, Everson Museum of Art, and the Canal Museum, all of Syracuse.

I am indebted to Amy Doherty, Mary E. Parker, Mrs. L. P. Hilton, Doris Lawson, David L. Rowe, Coy L. Ludwig, Steven J. Roper, Eleanor Johnson, Violet Hosler, and particularly the late Carolyn Wright for sharing their expertise, advice, or historical knowledge.

Thanks are also due to the School of Architecture, Syracuse University, for the opportunity to use the rich resources of the Harley McKee

Collection, now housed in the George Arents Research Library. Serious students of the architecture of central New York will forever be indebted to McKee's pioneering work in local architectural history. Another invaluable resource has been the Onondaga Historical Association, whose files have provided a major portion of information about Russell's structures. Unfortunately, space does not allow acknowledgment of the many other historians and individuals who, collectively, have helped to make this book possible.

Finally, I would like to extend my heartfelt thanks to Richard T. Lafferty, Henry W. Schramm, and Robert Marino, whose continual encouragement and moral support have been exceptional.

A welcome by-product of both the exhibition and this book would be the successful adaptive reuse of those Russell buildings which now stand empty. If this book can inspire continued, active pride in a regional heritage, then our efforts will have been amply rewarded.

Fall 1980 J. Brad Benson

Fourth Onondaga County Courthouse (1904–1907),
Syracuse, New York.

INTRODUCTION

Archimedes Russell had the good fortune to practice when he did, 1862–1915, and where he did, the central New York area, because the region experienced great growth during the span of his professional lifetime. Born in 1840 in Andover, Massachusetts, where his father was a builder, Russell was apprenticed to a sign painter, 1853–55. He also worked as a carpenter for his father.

Russell's architectural career began in 1860 when he started working for John Stevens, a Boston builder-architect. Russell's professional training through work with an established architect rather than attendance at a school of architecture was not unusual in a period when there were no American architectural schools and when very few aspiring architects studied in Europe. The builder-architect apprenticeship system was still strong. Because of a lull in commissions during the Civil War, Russell lost his job with Stevens in 1862 and came to Syracuse, where he found employment in the active office of Horatio Nelson White, a prominent Syracuse architect with whom he remained until he set up his own practice in 1868.

The 1868 census listed the population of Syracuse at 39,010, a substantial increase from the 1865 population of 31,774. There was an architectural boom in Syracuse with 850 new structures that year. It must have been a good time to begin a practice which was to include more than eight hundred commissions in a variety of styles before Russell's death in 1915. In addition to his busy practice, Russell found time from 1873 to 1881 to be an unpaid professor of architecture at Syracuse University, the third American university to offer formal architectural education.

Russell's office, like that of his Syracuse contemporaries Horatio Nelson White and Joseph Lyman Silsbee, was small, generally employing only one or two draftsmen. Asa L. Merrick worked for him 1870–77, and Charles E. Colton was in the office, 1875–78. Both Merrick and Colton later established their own firms. Melvin L. King began working for Russell in 1889 and became his partner in 1906, when Russell seems to have gone into semiretirement. After Russell's death, King took over the firm, which is now King & King Architects.

The period in which Russell worked, between the Civil War and the advent of World War I, was an age of eclecticism. American architects experimented with a variety of styles which provided a treasure trove of forms and details from the past. Russell, along with his local and national contemporaries, chose from such styles as High Victorian Gothic, Renaissance Revival, Romanesque Revival, Second Empire, Stick and Shingle, Queen Anne, Colonial Revival, Beaux-arts, and Mission as the century passed.

This plethora of stylistic modes presented the architect with so much choice that details often became mixed or seemed to overlap. While it is sometimes difficult to apply stylistic labels to buildings of the period, the mixture of architectural styles often added to the richness of the designs. Inspiration for designs might come from the *American Architect and Building News*, a periodical which began publication in 1876, or from the many American and European architectural books which architects of the time collected as source material.

Archimedes Russell was a regional architect; the majority of his work was in Syracuse, though he did work in some sixty central New York communities in thirteen counties. During the zenith of his career, from about 1885 to 1900, Syracuse experienced a doubling of population to 200,000 in 1900; in this period approximately half of his commissions were house designs. Russell may be considered a typical architect of his time in that he designed in the fashionable architectural trends, apparently well versed in those many styles developed by his more famous contemporaries on the national scene such as Richard Morris Hunt, Henry Hobson Richardson, and the members of the firm of McKim, Mead, and White.

A study of Russell's work informs us of general architectural developments in the United States before World War I. While some of his buildings have been demolished through the years, many still remain. They give human scale to our environment. They remind us of our past and the evolution of Syracuse as a city. A remembrance of those buildings which have been lost cautions us to guard those which fortunately still remain. A consideration of Russell's work forces us to think about our architectural past, present, and even our architectural future.

Mary Ann Smith

SECOND EMPIRE

The Second Empire mode came to the United States from France, where monumental buildings were being designed to impress the public and to represent the importance and elegance of the court of Napoleon III (1852– 70). The style seems to have crossed the Atlantic through the English architectural journals and books that kept American architects and builders informed about current developments abroad. A hallmark of the Second Empire style was the mansard roof—double pitched with a steep lower slope.

In Syracuse, the Hall of Languages (1871–73), Syracuse University's first building, was designed and built by Horatio Nelson White in the Second Empire style.

During the winter of 1868–69, Cornell University negotiated with Archimedes Russell, who produced a building which was stylistically a combination of Italian and French vocabularies, McGraw Hall (1869–72) (plate 1). The structure was built in three sections and was "substantially fireproof." The center section, four stories high, housed the museum, library (temporarily), and scientific collections in its large galleried hall. The flanking sections were used for lecture rooms, and the tower in the center held the chimes. The building of "Cornell quarry" blue sandstone is symmetrically arranged with a projecting center section higher than its two flanking sections. Rusticated quoins (rough-cut masonry blocks at the corners) articu-

CORNELL UNIVERSITY.

A. Russell.

1. McGraw Hall (1869–72), Cornell University, Ithaca, New York.
Courtesy of Department of Manuscripts and Archives, Cornell University.

late the façade. A stringcourse (continuous horizontal projecting ornamental band) unites the three parts of the center section and also separates the first floor from the upper three stories. All windows are round headed and carry Onondaga limestone voussoirs (wedge-shaped stones in the arch).

The building is symmetrical with mansard roofs of varying heights, punctuated by dormers, and topped by brick chimneys. The roof of the large tower in the center (plate 2) is pierced by small dormers and crowned by an ornamental cast and wrought iron cresting. Color was an important element in the Second Empire style, and Russell specified that the roofs were to be covered with Vermont slate of purple and green.

Iron columns were used for the construction of McGraw Hall. Wrought iron doors led from the library building to the other wings. The interior was finished in chestnut. Black walnut was used for stair rails, newel posts, and balusters. The interior was completed in 1872, and the building was renovated in 1964.

2. McGraw Hall, Tower.

VICTORIAN GOTHIC

The Gothic Revival came to the United States from England and was an outgrowth of the romantic movement in art and literature, which evoked nostalgic feelings about the Christian medieval past. Sir Walter Scott extolled the beauties of life in the Middle Ages in his writings and built Abbotsford, a "Scottish Baronial" house, at the beginning of the nineteenth century.

The Gothic Revival style is distinguished by the pointed arch, used in combination with towers, steep gable roofs, castellation (battlements and turrets), tracery, leaded and stained glass, foliated ornaments, and bargeboards. Plans are typically asymmetrical and the buildings often polychrome (multicolored).

Asymmetrical massing and the combination of a variety of forms were used not only in architecture but in landscape design as well. The wild, abundant American landscape was a particularly appropriate setting for the picturesque house. The idea that house and landscape are inseparable was successfully publicized by landscape architect Andrew Jackson Downing and architect Alexander Jackson Davis, whose collaboration in the 1840s and 50s produced a number of architectural books as well as picturesque villas and Gothic cottages.

Syracuse had its share of Gothic Revival buildings by noted architects. A splendid example of a castellated medieval dwelling, Yates Castle was designed by James Renwick and built in Syracuse, 1852–53. Alexander Jackson Davis also left his imprint on the central New York area with the now-demolished Sedgwick cottage on James Street in Syracuse (1845), and the Reuel Smith House in Skaneateles (1849–52).

Architectural books and journals which had been so important to the proliferation of architectural styles, especially during the second half of the nineteenth century, also played an essential role in advocating and publicizing a return to Gothic forms in church building. A reform movement within the established church in England led to the founding of the Ecclesiological Society in England and to a parallel development in America, the New York Ecclesiological Society. Both were concerned with the reform of the liturgy and of church building, advocating a return to the Gothic as the "true Christian style."

Horatio Nelson White, who had been a contractor for Yates Castle also built several Gothic Revival churches. The "Norman Gothic" Central Baptist Church at the corner of Jefferson and Montgomery Streets in Syracuse had probably been planned when Russell was still working in White's office, since excavation had begun as early as 1868. White also built Grace Episcopal Church (1876–77) at the corner of Madison Street and University Avenue in Syracuse. These were some of the Gothic Revival examples that Archimedes Russell would have known directly.

The Gothic Revival was a popular mode for mausoleums: the General Granger Mausoleum (1870) in Oakwood Cemetery, Syracuse, is an example (plate 3). Many materials were combined in this relatively small mausoleum. The base is of Onondaga gray limestone. Smoothly polished columns of Scotch granite rise from the limestone plinths (bases). From its foliated marble capitals spring two pointed arches. The structure is of blue and white

3. **General Granger Mausoleum (1870), Oakwood Cemetery, Syracuse, New York.**

Ohio sandstone. Rusticated stone in the pediment is pierced by a circular opening with a dripstone molding.

One of Russell's Gothic Revival churches is the Park Central Presbyterian Church (1871–75) on Townsend and Fayette Streets in Syracuse (plate 4). Here the massing is similar to his later Romanesque Revival churches—the basic box with two towers of differing height flanking the main façade (see plates 5 and 10)—although Russell paid obeisance to the Gothic by puncturing the walls with pointed arched openings decorated with quatrefoil tracery, lancet (narrow pointed arched) windows, and buttressing which here is ornamental rather than structural. St. Lucy's Roman Catholic Church (1873–75) on Gifford Street in Syracuse (plate 5) is similar in design to Park Central Presbyterian Church, with only slight variations. Pressed brick and limestone were used as building materials. The interior was renovated in the 1950s, and small exterior changes were made.

The High Victorian Gothic advocated by John Ruskin in his *Seven Lamps of Architecture* (1849) differed from the Gothic Revival mainly by being polychrome, a feature successfully employed in Joseph Lyman Silsbee's Syracuse Savings Bank (1876), and by detailing which is heavier than the fragile ornamentation used in Gothic Revival structures. The High Victorian Gothic style was used for churches as well as for public buildings, such as Russell's Hickok Building (1877) (plate 6).

One of Russell's Gothic Revival churches, the Camillus Baptist Church (1879–80) (plate 7), is pictured in Marcus Whiffin's *American Architecture since 1780: A Guide to the Styles* (Cambridge: MIT Press, 1969). Whiffin lists it as a good example of the High Victorian Gothic style, whose most important proponent in Britain had been William Butterfield, architect of the Church of All Saints, Margaret Street, London.

Elements of the High Victorian Gothic style in the Camillus Baptist

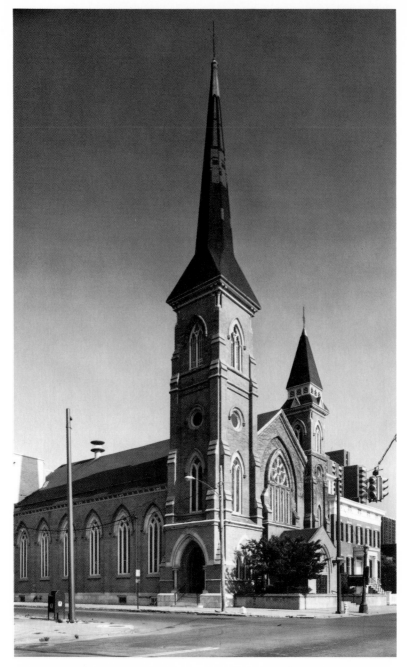

4. PARK CENTRAL PRESBYTERIAN CHURCH (1871–75), Grape (now Townsend) and Fayette Streets, Syracuse, New York. Altered.

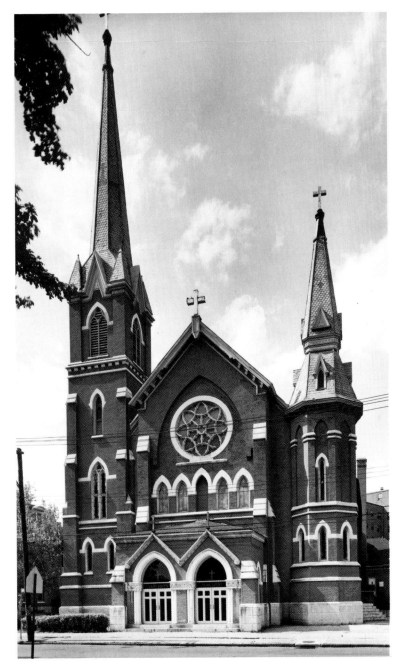

5. ST. LUCY'S ROMAN CATHOLIC CHURCH (1873–75), 432 Gifford Street,
Syracuse, New York.

BUILDING · CORNER OF NORTH SALINA AND CHURCH STS. SYRACUSE.

ARCHIMEDES RUSSELL ARCHT.

Church are the overall solidity of the building, windows set back into the walls, and the complex roofline accentuated by a single square tower on the west façade. A steeply pitched roof covers the rectangular main part of the church, and a small steeple projects from the rear. An eastern porch identifies the side entrance, and a five-cornered roof protects the bay window which is attached to the tower. The entrance porch facing the street is covered by a pitched roof which flares on each side into a shed roof.

Materials of different colors and textures are used to create interesting effects. Light-colored sandstone window sills and belt courses (projecting narrow horizontal bands defining interior floor levels) in the tower, and woodwork painted white contrast with the red brick of the walls. The focal point is the main entrance porch (plate 8), which is supported by polished stone columns with richly foliated acanthus (a plant with scalloped leaves) capitals. The geometric designs of the wrought iron grate in the entrance arch and in the stained glass windows replace the diaper work (patterned surface decoration) so often used in buildings of the High Victorian Gothic style. The assemblage is crowned by the white woodwork in the gable end of the entrance porch and, two stages above, by the woodwork in the gable of the main roof. The design of tie-beam and arched brace in the gable repeats that of the open timber roof in the interior. The woodwork of the porches, with its

6. **Hickok (or Hickox) Building (1877), North Salina and Church Streets, Syracuse, New York.** Demolished. More florid in its design than the McCarthy & Son Building (plate 39), this five-story commercial building was a free mixture of High Victorian Gothic and Queen Anne elements. Among the unique features were piers, (vertical structural supports) that seemed to continue beyond the roofline as chimneys ornamented with gargoyles. Flower garlands filled the segmental arches (less than a semicircle), which were supported by iron columns on the first floor store front facing Salina Street. This perspective drawing was published in *The American Architect and Building News*, October 1, 1877. The building was razed in 1973.

8. CAMILLUS BAPTIST CHURCH, Main Entrance Porch.

7. CAMILLUS BAPTIST CHURCH (1879–80), Genesee Street, Camillus, New York.

squares, cinquefoil, semicircular, and diamond-shaped cutouts, suggests the geometric rigor of the total plan. A pamphlet in the archives of the church describes the plan as follows:

> Mr. Russell employed mathematical and geometric designs to achieve the excellent and pleasing proportions of our church. He used the circle and square design method. The entire structure of the Camillus Baptist Church in cross section from the church floor to the highest visible element at the ridge and from the outside wall to inside wall, forms an exact square. Dividing this basic square into quarters, each another perfect square, pinpoints the bottom most member of the church framework. Two adjoining squares inside the church locate the intersection of the roof and sidewalls. The circle and square methods were used by Mr. Russell to proportion the stair tower and entrances and were even incorporated in the stained glass windows in the nave, narthex, stair tower and the parish hall. The stained glass windows of the Gothic period are quite simple, though geometrically magnificent, and are intertwined with acanthus leaves.

The auditorium was frescoed and finished in ash and walnut. In 1968 the church was struck by lightning and was almost destroyed. Careful restoration and several interior changes have made the church functional once more.

Russell also designed the Otsego County Courthouse, Cooperstown (1880) (plate 9) in the High Victorian Gothic style; St. Peter's Roman Catholic Church, Rome (1894–95) (plates 10, 11) and the First Methodist Episcopal Church, Syracuse (1903–1904) (plate 12), were built in the Victorian Gothic mode.

9. OTSEGO COUNTY COURTHOUSE (1880), 193 Main Street, Cooperstown, New York. A richly textured and polychrome exterior surface, Queen Anne details (a sunflower actually emerges from the peak of the roof!), a combination of round headed, pointed, and trabeated windows (designed with posts and beams, or lintels), and an asymmetrical massing make this building a striking example of Russell's fondness for eclectic modes. The courthouse is listed on the National Register of Historic Places. *Photo courtesy of George Arents Research Library, Syracuse University.*

11. St. Peter's Roman Catholic Church. Gilded ribs articulate the vaulted ceiling.

10. St. Peter's Roman Catholic Church (1894–95), North James and East Park Streets, Rome, New York. This is the largest church Russell designed. Medina cut stone with brown sandstone was used for the exterior. Polygonal spires top exterior towers, both of which are visually supported by buttressing. The large tower features corbel tables and spire lights. The church is entered through three large pointed arched portals. Fine stained glass windows depict Biblical scenes. In the 1960s the exterior was cleaned and repainted, and the interior has been renovated.

12. First Methodist Episcopal Church (1903–1904), East Onondaga, State, and East Jefferson Streets, Syracuse, New York. Demolished. The rustication of the stone and the three crenellated (notched) towers gave the church a solid, fortresslike appearance. The overall design seemed well suited to the building site. The polygonal shape carried the building around the corner and turned the eye smoothly toward the smaller tower, along East Onondaga Street toward Columbus Circle. The church burned in 1954. *Photo courtesy of J. Brad Benson.*

VICTORIAN ITALIANATE

The Italianate style, popular in the United States during the second half of the nineteenth century, was an eclectic style notable for its square plan, low-pitched roof, overhanging bracketed eaves, entrance tower, round-headed windows with hood moldings, quoins, balustraded balconies, cupolas, lanterns, and arcaded porches.

Residences in the Victorian Italianate style proliferated in Syracuse as they did elsewhere in the country. An example is St. John the Evangelist Rectory, designed by Archimedes Russell in 1874 (plate 13). The principal façade is symmetrical; three-story bays flank a two-tiered porch in the center. The first story is lighted by tall narrow windows in groups of three with projecting hood moldings (or dripstones). The segmental arch (less than a semi-circle) is used over the main entrance and the porch window above. A segmental arch also tops the second-story bay windows. Trabeated windows (designed with posts and beams, or lintels) give light to the third floor and are also employed on the side façades. The windows of each level are proportionally smaller than their counterparts on the floor below. The lantern, which is placed in the center of the low-pitched hip roof, is pierced by small round headed windows in groups of three on all four sides. Chimneys placed near each of the four corners emphasize the symmetry of the main part of the house, which is almost square in plan. A two-story addition that has a

13. RECTORY, ST. JOHN the EVANGELIST ROMAN CATHOLIC CHURCH (1874), North State and Willow Streets, Syracuse, New York.

separate round arched entrance and trabeated windows abuts the back. The two bays and the porch lend a "baroque" plasticity to the main façade. It is likely that the second-story porch front was originally open and was later enclosed. Heavy paired brackets underneath the wide eaves, ornamental corbelled (supported by projecting blocks) hood moldings with heavy keystones, paired pillars flanking the main entrance and porch windows, and a decorative frieze below the porch window are typically used in Victorian Italianate houses. Over the years, some interior changes have been made in this house, which is still used as a rectory and church office.

ROMANESQUE REVIVAL

The Middle Ages provided the prototypes favored for church building during much of the second half of the nineteenth century. The Romanesque Revival or round arched style, which Russell used for Crouse Memorial College (1887–89) (plate 14), vied with the pointed arched Gothic Revival style for popularity.

Henry Hobson Richardson, while studying at the École des beaux-arts in Paris, became intrigued by the Romanesque buildings of southern France and northern Spain. He thought the Romanesque to be the most proper source of inspiration for architects and developed his version of the Romanesque Revival style in America. The overall effect of his buildings depended on mass, volume, scale, and materials rather than surface decoration. In his *Hints on Architecture* (1847–48) Robert Owen had urged the use of the Romanesque Revival style for secular architecture of which James Renwick's Smithsonian Institution (1846–49) was the first famous example.

In Syracuse the Romanesque Revival style became very popular. Horatio Nelson White built three round arched churches during the period 1862–68, the years that Archimedes Russell was working for him. Between 1871 and 1891 Russell built several Romanesque Revival churches and public buildings in and around Syracuse. In most cases he used a rectangular floor plan, the basic box. Round headed windows and doors puncture the mono-

14. CROUSE MEMORIAL COLLEGE (1887–89), Syracuse University, Syracuse, New York, South Entrance.

chrome brick or stone walls, corbel tables enhance the eaves, and belt courses mark horizontal divisons. Main façades are flanked by polygonal or circular towers of unequal height. Frequently, blind arcades (a set of arches set against or recessed in a wall) ornament exterior walls. Romanesque Revival buildings conveyed solidity and strength, and it was claimed that they were not only durable but that they could be erected quickly and economically.

A good example of the use of Romanesque for public buildings was Archimedes Russell's County Clerk's Office (1880–81) (plates 15, 16). It was constructed of brick; the floors were supported by iron beams and columns; its doors, window frames, sashes, and stairway were of iron; it had a corrugated iron roof. In short, it was to be as fireproof as possible. When it was finished in 1881, the new county building was hailed by the local press as being the finest in central New York. When in 1960 the Public Safety Building was scheduled to replace this "dirty brick monument to antiquity," as the Syracuse *Post-Standard* later described it on December 29, 1963, the structure was razed despite efforts to save it.

One of Russell's Syracuse buildings that may be termed Richardsonian Romanesque is Syracuse University's Crouse Memorial College (1887–89) (plates 14, 17–19). The building was a gift to Syracuse University from John Crouse and his son, D. Edgar Crouse, the richest men in Syracuse at that time. John Crouse insisted that the building be called "Crouse Memorial College for Women," and those words are inscribed above its door. The Crouse College building opened as the new home of the College of Fine Arts. It was the third building on campus, following Horatio Nelson White's Hall of Languages (1871–73), the first campus building, and Holden Observatory (1887).

The commanding hill on which Crouse College was to stand looked down upon Chestnut Street, soon to become Crouse Avenue. The construc-

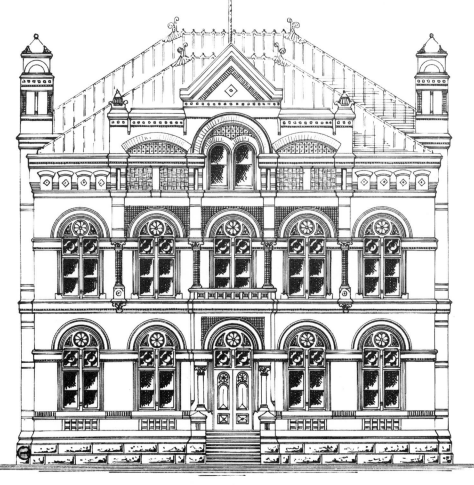

Church Street Front.

SCALE ½ INCH.

16. COUNTY CLERK'S OFFICE. Demolished. *Photo courtesy of Onondaga County Public Library.*

15. COUNTY CLERK'S OFFICE (1880–81), Church and Clinton Streets, Syracuse, New York. *Elevation courtesy of George Arents Research Library, Syracuse University.*

tion contract had been awarded to Norcross Brothers of Worcester, Massachusetts, a firm that had built several of Richardson's buildings. The organization of the windows on the east and west façades of Crouse College—basement, two stories, and balcony level, grouped vertically under four arches—points to several Richardson buildings whose façades were articulated in the same manner. The combination of trabeated windows—in Crouse College used in the basement and first floor levels—with round headed windows in the upper two levels, as well as the steep gabled dormers, are also part of the Richardsonian vocabulary. The asymmetrical plan, square and polygonal bays, a large tower, the use of pilasters (shallow piers attached to a wall), rounded corbelled turrets, chimneys, and small towers growing out of the hipped roof emphasize the plasticity as well as the picturesque quality of the edifice (plate 17).

The façades of Crouse College are richly ornamented, especially with a stylized sunflower motif of terra cotta in gables, pediments, and elaborately carved capitals, and in the interior on ornate newel posts. Russell was fond of this symbol and used it in many of his buildings in the 1880s, particularly in his Queen Anne houses. Entrances on the north and south façades are surrounded by elaborate stone carvings. Gables, turrets, and chimneys are adorned with blind arcades. A spiral motif, marking the second and third levels, runs along the east façade but does not appear on the west side. Three niches are carved into the lower part of the tower. They are empty, but they might have been intended to house pieces of scuplture.

The main entrance is on the north side through the tower (plate 18) and is connected by a long corridor to another entrance on the south side opposite it. The grand staircase connecting the first, second, and third floors was originally planned in marble. However, after John Crouse's death, shortly before it could be installed, his son, D. Edgar, changed the material to wood

17. CROUSE MEMORIAL COLLEGE. *Photo courtesy of George Arents Research Library, Syracuse University.*

19. CROUSE MEMORIAL COLLEGE, Interior. Auditorium with Holtkamp organ.

18. CROUSE MEMORIAL COLLEGE, North Entrance.

for reasons of economy. On the second floor the Grand Memorial Music Hall (now Crouse College Auditorium) seats twelve hundred people (plate 19). It was also used for chapel services until Hendricks Chapel was built. The appearance of a church interior was conveyed by an open timber roof seventy feet high and by stained glass windows ending in arches above a balcony supported by slender cast iron columns with ornate capitals. The design of the stained glass is geometric; circles, squares, and fan-shaped motifs are prevalent.

The Roosevelt organ, a gift of John Crouse, was replaced in 1950 by the much larger Holtkamp organ. During the 1950s, cracks appeared in the plaster above the organ alcove, a space that had been ornamented with a peacock design. This design unfortunately was painted over when the damage was repaired. Old photographs show that the stage was originally smaller than it is now. The frosted glass that fills the transoms in the doors along the corridors was imported from Italy. The design of the glass differs slightly on each floor.

20. **UNIVERSITY AVENUE METHODIST EPISCOPAL CHURCH (1871−72), East Genesee Street and University Avenue, Syracuse, New York.** The building was constructed of pressed brick with stone trim. The auditorium, supported by iron columns, was frescoed in pastel colors. Light filtered through stained glass windows. On the exterior round headed windows and portals were capped with heavy hood moldings with corbel stops and large keystones. The main entrances were in the two towers of differing height which culminated in four-cornered spires. *Photo from* Syracuse Illustrated, 1890, *courtesy of Onondaga County Public Library*.

In 1973 four fused glass windows by Professor Richard Wolff of the School of Art were installed in the north entrance. In the early 1970s the building was renovated, and it was entered on the National Register of Historic Places in 1974.

Russell's first Romanesque church, the University Avenue Methodist Episcopal Church (plates 20–22), was built in 1871–72 on the northwest corner of East Genesee Street and University Avenue in Syracuse. Russell's fondness for the Romanesque Revival even as late as the 1890s is shown in the Von Ranke Library, Syracuse (1888–89) (plate 23); James Stevens House, Rome (1890) (plates 24–27); the Delaware Street Baptist Church, Syracuse (1890–97) (plate 28); and St. Anthony of Padua Convent and Church (1896–97, 1911) (plates 29–31).

21. **UNIVERSITY AVENUE METHODIST EPISCOPAL CHURCH.** In 1914 a fire destroyed the building.

22. **UNIVERSITY AVENUE METHODIST EPISCOPAL CHURCH.** A large fresco painting of a room opening up behind the altar which visually enlarged the auditorium was destroyed in the 1914 fire.

23. **Von Ranke Library (now Administration Building) (1888–89), Syracuse University, Syracuse, New York.** Altered. The interior was made as nearly fireproof as possible with bookcases built of gas pipe as well as angle iron and with an iron staircase. The exterior is of Trenton brick dressed with terra cotta. The relationship between Crouse College (plate 17) and the Von Ranke Library was made clear by the use of much of the same architectural and stylistic vocabulary in both buildings. The original structure was asymmetrical; when the west wing was added in 1906 the building became symmetrical. At that time the books were moved to Carnegie Library, and the Von Ranke Library became Syracuse University's Administration Building. *Photo courtesy of George Arents Research Library, Syracuse University.*

24. JAMES STEVENS HOUSE (1890), Embargo and Washington Streets, Rome, New York. The influence of Henry Hobson Richardson and his contemporaries is evident in this fine stone mansion. During the 1880s, many of these massive, vigorously formed stone houses were built throughout the country. The Stevens house is built of Potsdam red sandstone which is finished with Longmeadow brown sandstone and rests upon a foundation of white granite. The heavy stone massing and a large round corner tower convey a feeling of stability. The house has been used as a VFW building since 1945. Since then the house has undergone exterior and interior changes.

25. JAMES STEVENS HOUSE, Ceiling Detail.

26. JAMES STEVENS HOUSE, Fire-place. Russell collaborated with Hart Brothers of New York City in designing the interior. The hearth of the fireplace, located in what was once the music room, features a lyre design in the mosaic.

27. JAMES STEVENS HOUSE, Ceiling Painting. Painted on canvas by Kellar of New York City.

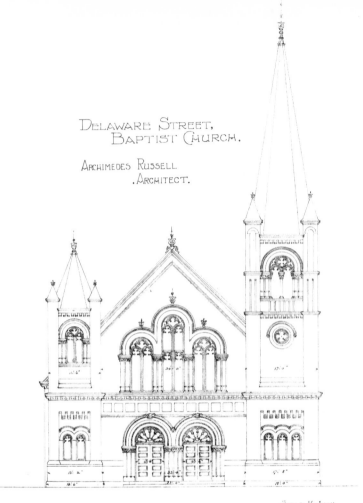

DELAWARE STREET,
BAPTIST CHURCH.

ARCHIMEDES RUSSELL
.ARCHITECT.

SCALE ⅛ INCH.

DELAWARE ST. ELEVATION.

28. DELAWARE STREET BAPTIST CHURCH (1890–97), Dudley and Delaware Streets, Syracuse, New York. Altered. Classical details such as pilasters, columns, dentils beneath the belt course, and the egg and dart molding are the same Russell used in many of the residences he designed during the 1890s. In 1958 a fire destroyed much of the two older wings. The interior was gutted and completely refinished by the Syracuse architectural firm of Sargent Webster Crenshaw & Folley. *Elevation courtesy of George Arents Research Library, Syracuse University.*

29. S⒯. A⒩⒯⒣⒪⒩⒴ of P⒜⒟⒰⒜ C⒪⒩⒱⒠⒩⒯ (1896–97), Court Street, Syracuse, New York. The convent is still used and stands surrounded by a landscaped garden. The building is symmetrically designed with a centrally placed round arched entrance. A projecting midsection is flanked by rounded buttresses which are repeated rhythmically on both wings and on the other façades. *Photo courtesy of Onondaga Historical Association.*

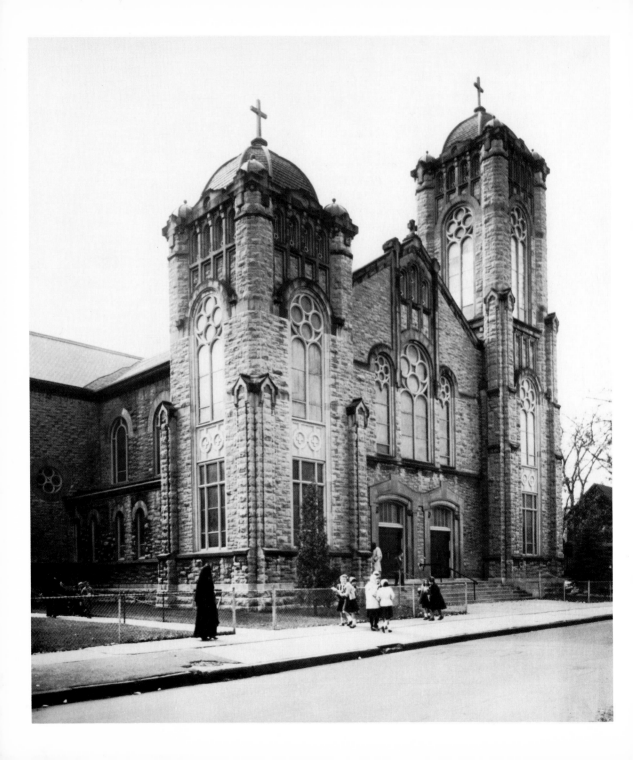

31. St. Anthony of Padua Church, Interior. Originally the interior was painted in soft shades of green and gray. Now the vaulted plaster ceiling and walls are painted to resemble the interior of Renaissance churches. The circular ornamentation is prevalent throughout.

30. St. Anthony of Padua Church (1911), Midland Avenue and Colvin Street, Syracuse, New York. The remarkable growth of the Catholic population of Syracuse led to the division of St. Mary's (established in 1841) and the formation of the new parish of St. Anthony of Padua on the south side of the city during the first decade of the twentieth century. The church pamphlet hails its "beautiful marble church." Marble was indeed used for the altars, the sanctuary railing, and the pulpit. The exterior, asymmetrically massed, was constructed of rusticated stone with limestone trim. The plan is that of a Greek cross. A large square tower anchors the building at the corner of Midland Avenue and Colvin Street. Unlike Russell's other Romanesque churches, here all of the towers are crowned by cupolas. *Photo courtesy of St. Anthony of Padua Church.*

STICK STYLE

The Stick style together with the Shingle style may be considered the most American of all the nineteenth-century styles, despite their indebtedness to the wooden houses of Switzerland, southern Germany, and Italy. The principal characteristic of the Stick style was the expression of the structure of the house through the exterior ornament—usually a series of intersecting boards (sticks) applied over the surface to symbolize the structural skeleton.

Archimedes Russell received the commission for Hamilton S. White's firehouse in 1878 (plate 32). The elegant three-story frame firehouse was erected at 124 East Genesee Street. "Chemical No. 2," as it was referred to, was both built and maintained by Hamilton White at his own expense. Its exterior exhibited a multitude of Stick style elements. A skin of narrow clapboards stretched across the structural skeleton. On the entrance façade porch posts with diagonal bracing supported a second-floor balcony. The three-part roof system of the porch was supported by posts with diagonal, slightly curved bracing. In the gable of the main façade and in the cross gable, Russell punctured the walls with ribbon windows. According to the *Syracuse Daily Standard* of January 3, 1879, the front and the rear façades of the fire engine house had triple windows of extra-heavy French plate glass with a single light to each sash. Above each upper sash a transom window was

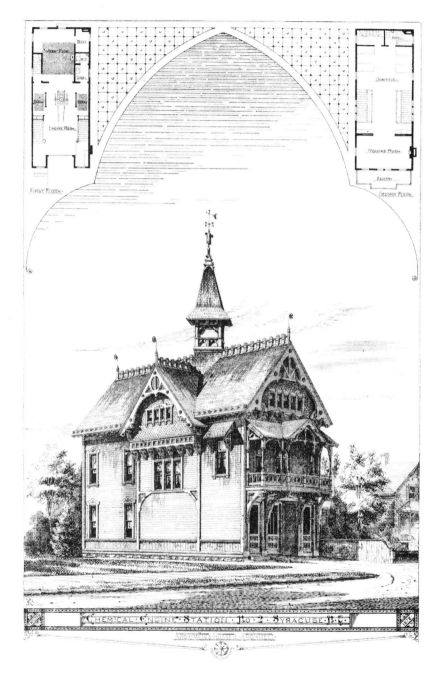

32. HAMILTON S. WHITE CHEMICAL ENGINE HOUSE (1878), 124 East Genesee Street, Syracuse, New York. Demolished.

decorated with colored glass. Beneath the balcony two large double sash doors, wide enough to allow the fire engines to go through, closed the main entrance to the engine house. This entrance was flanked by doors for occupants and visitors. The cross gable was balanced on the west façade by a tall chimney of Philadelphia pressed brick pointed in white. The exterior woodwork was painted a dark color. A small tower, which accommodated the electrical connections with the fire alarm and the district telegraphs, sat in the center of the roof. Its roof was supported by a system of vertical posts with bracings and horizontal sticks. The cresting, the stick work, and the cut-out ornaments in the cross and the main gables gave the structure a lacy fairy-talelike appearance thoroughly belying its function.

But functional it was. The first floor included commodious box stalls for two horses. The "well-ventilated" stalls, padded on the sides with Brussels carpeting, were provided with sectioned rack flooring that carried waste materials directly to the city sewers. On the second floor the "most complete bath in the city," a billiard table, and an elegantly furnished reading room warmed by a fireplace with a carved cherry and ebony mantle helped to while away the fireman's time when he was not fighting fires.

To assure that the firemen, cozy in this luxurious setting, would also respond quickly to the call of duty, cords over the front of each bunkbed, running through holes in the ceiling and attached to the bedding, snatched the bedding up to the ceiling as soon as the alarm was sounded. The entire third floor was given over to the water tank.

The "model and palatial building" had been erected for the cost of $30,000 and was ready for occupany on January 1, 1879. Hamilton S. White, who died while fighting a fire in the city, willed the building to the city. Years later the structure had to be reinforced when motorized firefighting equipment was installed, and it was finally demolished around 1915.

33. WESTMINSTER PRESBYTERIAN CHURCH (1886), Douglas and Graves Streets, Syracuse, New York. Altered. The foundation of this wood structure was laid in 1886, but the church was not dedicated until 1891. Russell designed it in the Stick style and employed classical and Queen Anne details. The plan of the church and its massing are irregular. A skin of clapboards stretches across the skeleton of the structure. Vertical sticks sharply emphasize all corners as well as window and door frames. The square tower is topped by an open belfry. Its polygonal roof is held by sticklike supports, and its balustrade consists of diagonal stick work. The pediment of the Neoclassical window on the south side features Eastlake ornamentation. The building houses the Zonta Girls' Club and is being renovated. *Photo from* Protestant & Protestant Episcopal Churches in Syracuse, N.Y., *1895, Geddes Congregational Church.*

34. WILLIAM KELLOGG HOUSE (1889), 22 North Main Street, Homer, New York. Altered. In this two-story wood frame house the sunflower motif is prominently featured in gables, windows, doors, balustrade, and even on the weathervane. This asymmetrically planned Stick style home has an irregular roofline. The interior is decorated with fine woods, parquetry, and stained glass windows. *Photo courtesy of Thomas and Ruth Haskell.*

Russell also employed the Stick style in the Westminster Presbyterian Church, Syracuse (1886) (plate 33), and in the William Kellogg House, Homer (1889) (plates 34–37).

35. WILLIAM KELLOGG HOUSE, Gable End with Sunflower Motif. *Photo courtesy of J. Brad Benson.*

36. WILLIAM KELLOGG HOUSE, Front (East) Elevation. *Courtesy of Thomas and Ruth Haskell.*

37. WILLIAM KELLOGG HOUSE, Side (South) Elevation. *Courtesy of Thomas and Ruth Haskell.*

QUEEN ANNE

In America, Queen Anne style meant a free eclectic contrast of textural surfaces and materials and the employment of classical ornament on basically medieval forms. Marcus Whiffin notes in his *American Architecture since 1780* that the well-known nineteenth-century architectural critic Montgomery Schuyler was severely critical of this eclecticism and suggested that the proponents of the style were to be considered "the extreme left, a frantic and vociferous mob, who welcomed the new departure as the dis-establishment of all standards, whether of authority or of reason, and as an emancipation of all restraints, even those of public decency." And when English architect Charles L. Eastlake, whose *Hints on Household Taste* (1878) had become very popular in the United States, gave Queen Anne his nod of approval, the new style had arrived.

In Syracuse, as elsewhere in the country, architects and builders jumped into the fray almost as vociferously as Montgomery Schuyler had claimed. Not least among them was Archimedes Russell, whose fondness for the sunflower symbol has already been mentioned in connection with Crouse College. The sunflower vogue had been started in England by William Morris and by some of the pre-Raphaelites. These ubiquitous flowers, together with towers, bulbous bays, chimneys, the textural wall (occasionally complemented by colored glass panels in the windows), and a variety of forms and colors, were external manifestations of the Queen Anne style which were widely used by American architects like Russell. One of the most important features of the style, however, the Queen Anne living hall, which served as the core of the house and which had been one of Richardson's contributions to American domestic architecture, is not found in Russell's houses.

One of Russell's most lavish Queen Anne buildings, at least as far as the interior was concerned, was the D. Edgar Crouse stables that he designed and constructed in 1887–88 (plate 38 and back cover). During the same time, he built Crouse College as well as the Von Ranke Library on the Syracuse University campus, and there is noticeable similarity among all three buildings.

In the Crouse stables there was a preponderance of gables, dormers, and ornate corbelled chimney stacks, along with a steeply pitched roof topped with wrought iron cresting, and round and polygonal gables. The Queen Anne sunflower symbol was everywhere: in the semicircular tympanums (the area within an arch above a lintel) surrounded by stone voussoirs above the windows, in terra cotta plaques on the main chimney, above the doorway in a band around the corbelling of the chimney, arranged like small flags throughout the façade of the main gable, and in a band between the first and second floor levels placed underneath each glazed opening like exclamation points. Here, as in Crouse College, trabeated windows are combined with semicircular openings. When the $200,000 structure was finished in the spring of 1888, D. Edgar and his horses moved into a truly elegant abode. D. Edgar's steeds lived in rosewood stalls, they drank from brass trimmed porcelain bowls, and they exercised in a large court covered with a skylight. Herter Brothers of New York, personal designers for the Vanderbilts, had lavishly designed the rest of the interior.

Apparently D. Edgar was a misogynistic bachelor, and he shared his

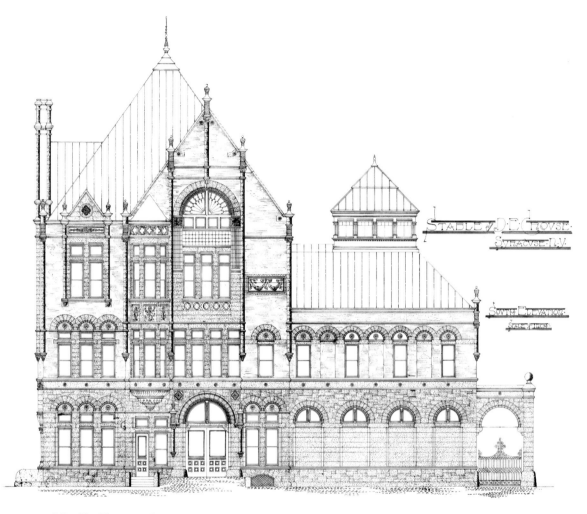

38. D. Edgar Crouse Stables (1887–88), Mulberry and South Streets (now East Fayette and State Streets), Syracuse, New York. Demolished.
Elevation courtesy of George Arents Research Library, Syracuse University.

sumptuous surroundings with his horses and his servants. However, after his death in 1892, a Viennese baroness appeared in Syracuse accompanied by a little girl named D. Edgarita who, the mother claimed, was the daughter of D. Edgar. The family was touched, and Edgarita and her mother were given two million dollars and sent back to Europe.

Later D. Edgar's house was stripped of much of its oriental splendor. After it had served as a clubhouse for the Syracuse Athletic Association, Gustav Stickley occupied the building for some time, and it was then called the "Craftsman Building." For a while it housed the Independent Telephone Company and the New York Telephone Company, and later offices for unemployment relief. When it seemed impossible to find any use for the "old barn" the building was demolished in 1936.

Between 1876 and 1885, Archimedes Russell designed five business structures and a residence that could loosely be labeled Queen Anne in their massing and use of details: the McCarthy Building, Syracuse (1876–77) (plate 39); the Hickok Building, Syracuse (1877) (plate 6); the Howard Soule House, Syracuse (1877) (plate 40); the Francis Hendricks Building, Syracuse (1878–79) (plate 41); the Pulaski National Bank, Pulaski (1882) (plate 42); and the Third National Bank, Syracuse (1885–86) (plate 43).

In 1876 Dennis McCarthy, the owner of a prospering wholesale house which had outgrown its previous quarters, commissioned Russell to design and build the new McCarthy Building on the corner of Washington and Clinton Streets in Syracuse (plate 39). This was an excellent location contiguous to several railroad depots. In January 1877, the building was ready for occupancy. It was basically a flat-roofed Renaissance block with Queen Anne and High Victorian Gothic ornamentation such as diapering in the gables, the ubiquitous sunflower motif, and the use of building materials of different colors. On January 4, 1877, the Syracuse *Journal* described the

39. McCarthy Building (1876–77), Washington and Clinton Streets, Syracuse, New York. *Elevation courtesy of George Arents Research Library, Syracuse University.*

building in detail. It is interesting to note that the main emphasis in the article was on the description of the structure, a fact which suggests growing awareness of new building methods and materials. The McCarthy Building was one of the earliest buildings in Syracuse to have a steam-powered (Otis) elevator. After the Syracuse Savings Bank (1876) was constructed with a passenger elevator, no commercial building could afford to be without one. The McCarthy structure was razed in 1973.

Around 1870 Syracuse had thirteen banks. In the early 1870s business in Syracuse so attracted the commercial world that the *New York Times* sent a reporter to write about it. Between 1860 and 1870, the city's wealth had more than quadrupled, and there had been an increase of a thousand buildings in one year, as Franklin Henry Chase noted in his *Syracuse and Its Environs* (New York: Lewis, 1924).

The Third National Bank was the first commercial bank in Syracuse to erect its own building (plate 43), first in 1885, rebuilt in 1912; an addition on the north side facing Salina Street was constructed in 1926. With its gables, dormers, trabeated and round headed windows, its sunflowers and "pie" motifs, this building exhibits Russell's fondness for the Queen Anne mode. A Gothic trefoil over the side door on James Street is filled with carved sunflowers. The materials used were Trenton pressed brick and Carlisle red sandstone. The addition of 1926 was carefully designed to complement the existing structure. In 1972 the building was entered on the National Register of Historic Places. With its neighbors, the Syracuse Savings Bank and the old Onondaga County Savings Bank (the Gridley Building), the Third National Bank shows the magnitude of Syracuse commerce in the late nineteenth century.

40. HOWARD SOULE HOUSE (1877), 174 James Street, Syracuse, New York.
Demolished. On December 1, 1877, the *American Architect and Building News*
published this perspective of a house built by Archimedes Russell for Howard
Soule, a city engineer. A photograph taken by Harley McKee before its
demolition in 1962 shows the house with a mansard roof and a main entrance
sheltered by a barrel vaulted roof supported by pillars and without a tower. It
was one of the last of the great James Street mansions, with an interior that
could boast of fireplaces bordered with Majolica and Minton tiles, a vaulted
wine cellar, an Italian tiled fountain, and a gymnasium on the top floor.

41. FRANCIS HENDRICKS BUILDING (1878–79), East Fayette Street and Bank Alley, Syracuse, New York. Altered. This commercial building is located on the site of the former home of Harvey Baldwin, first mayor of Syracuse. Here, as in the McCarthy Building (plate 39), much attention was paid by the local papers to mechanical contrivances and utilities, such as hydraulic elevators, dumb waiters, radiators, and elegant gas fixtures. In 1879 the Bryant Library, a circulating library cum bookstore and reading rooms, moved into part of the building. Russell's drawing for the front elevation featured segmental arches of the store fronts (supported by cast iron centers), fine brick work, including diapering, and Queen Anne style chimneys topped by turrets. In much altered form the building is still used for commercial purposes. *Photo courtesy of Holly Barlow Burns.*

42. PULASKI NATIONAL BANK (now LINCOLN FIRST BANK) (1882), Pulaski, New York. The building is constructed of red brick with Vermont marble trim. Queen Anne and High Victorian Gothic details combined with the polychromy of the façades make the exterior of this structure an interesting example of eclectic design. *Photo courtesy of Oswego Historical Society.*

43. THIRD NATIONAL BANK (1885–86), Salina and James Streets, Syracuse, New York. Altered. *Photo courtesy of Onondaga Historical Association.*

COLONIAL REVIVAL

The 1876 Centennial in Philadelphia gave impetus to a renewed interest in colonial styles. Architects in the East were inspired by houses built in the Georgian and Federal styles. Larger than these colonial houses, their Colonial Revival houses had symmetrical façades and rectangular plans with few projections. Colors are light; ornamentation takes its inspiration from the Adamesque style of a hundred years earlier; a Palladian window often becomes the focal point; broken swansneck ornamentation graces the front entrance; and the eaves of hipped or gambrel roofs feature classical detailing. The Colonial Revival became especially popular for suburban houses.

The George L. Gridley House on South Salina Street in Syracuse, which Russell designed and built in the Colonial Revival style in 1898, has a horizontality which is not as apparent in his earlier houses, along with classical detailing underneath the eaves of the hip roof and under the porch roof on the second level (plate 44).

The Charles Frank House on Danforth Street in Syracuse is a fine example of the Colonial Revival style (plate 45). It was finished in 1899 for George Zett, who lived next door in a house also designed by Russell in the same year (plate 46). Zett, a well-to-do brewer, had commissioned the house for his daughter and son-in-law. The house was constructed of Roman hydraulic brick with a base of cut blue Warsaw stone. Its gambrel roof was

44. GEORGE L. GRIDLEY HOUSE (1898), 1213 (now 1818) South Salina Street, Syracuse, New York. The site was originally part of the old Kirk Tract. The house was built for Dr. George L. Gridley, a physician who owned race horses kept in a barn, now gone, near the house. *Photo courtesy of Onondaga Historical Association.*

45. Charles A. Frank House (1899), 700 Danforth Street, Syracuse, New York.

covered with Spanish tiles. The house is almost rectangular in plan with minor projections on the sides. The main façade is symmetrical with a slightly projecting central part, vertically combining a semicircular entrance porch supported by paired columns, a Palladian window, and a classical pediment. Heavy quoins emphasize the corners. Stained glass windows were imported from Germany; bathroom tiles have eighteen carat gold decorations; there is finely carved woodwork on balusters and newel posts and an oval painting on the ceiling of the stairhall. Mosaic tiles form the initial "F" on the floor of the entranceway.

Russell also designed the Snowdon Apartment Building, Syracuse (1902–1904) (plate 47), using Colonial Revival details.

46. George Zett House (1899), 702 Danforth Street, Syracuse, New York.
The interior of this large and elegant house was finished in quartersawn white
oak. Plate glass and stained glass windows imported from Munich were used
throughout. Part of the basement was used as a bowling alley, and the house
was furnished with steam heat and electric light.

47. **SNOWDON APARTMENT BUILDING (1902–1904), James Street and Burnet Avenue, Syracuse, New York.** Walter Snowdon Smith built this apartment house, designed by Archimedes Russell. This six-story brick building, has two main wings with a wedge-shaped courtyard between them. Elements such as bowfronts, vertical rows of balconies with decorative wrought iron balusters, and a semicircular entrance porch supported by fluted composite columns, keystones, and voussoirs painted white combine to make the Snowdon a handsome edifice. After falling into disrepair, it was purchased by the Phelps Corporation which is restoring the building.

COMMERCIAL

Technological innovation brought about a uniquely American mode of building, the Commercial style. Cast iron fronts permitted large, open interior spaces, and buildings were made taller because of their use of the passenger elevator and less ornate because of the need for economy. In matters of mass and articulation, these precursors to the skyscraper looked back to Renaissance examples.

Archimedes Russell designed Syracuse's first "skyscraper" in 1887–88. Local people were mightily impressed with the Snow Building on Warren Street (plate 48). An eight-story wallbearing brick structure reinforced by steel beams, it towered above its four-story neighbors.

A few years later Russell returned to a sprawling horizontality with the construction of the Yates Hotel (1891–92) (plate 49) and the Dey Brothers Department Store (1893) (plate 50), both built in Syracuse. This horizontality echoed the development in other smaller cities in the East where real estate was not as expensive as in the larger metropolitan centers. Most commercial buildings stayed within the five- or six-story limit well after the 1870s.

The Yates Hotel was one of the most important commissions Russell received during his career. It was built in Syracuse on the corners of Washington, Genesee, Montgomery, and Fayette Streets with money from

48. C. W. Snow Building (1887–88), 216 South Warren Street, Syracuse, New York. Altered. *Photo courtesy of George Arents Research Library, Syracuse University.*

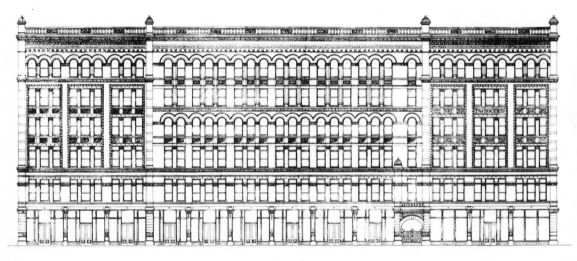

"THE YATES"
Archimēdes Russell, Architect

- MONTGOMERY STREET ELEVATION -
· SCALE ⅛ INCH ·

49. YATES HOTEL (1891–92), Washington, Genesee, Montgomery, and Fayette Streets, Syracuse, New York. Demolished. *Elevation courtesy of George Arents Research Library, Syracuse University.*

the estate of Alonzo Chester Yates, who had occupied Yates Castle. On a September night in 1892, the hotel opened with great festivity, and Syracusans were delighted with their new and splendid hotel. Its elegant interior was described in the local press in glowing terms. The fact that the interior included an electric light plant and an ice machine attracted much attention. It was also pointed out that first-class materials, such as rolled steel girders and cast iron fire separations, were used in the solid construction. Russell was quite concerned that the occupants of the Yates Hotel have complete fire protection. He suggested that more than one staircase be built. The owners objected, maintaining that the space was too valuable and that one staircase would do. A compromise was reached, and fire escapes were built on the exterior at the rear of the building.

The ground floor of the Yates Hotel was given over to stores. Special visual attention was paid to the second floor. It was separated from the first and the third floors by unbroken entablatures, with stringcourses connecting the upper part of the trabeated windows. Windows in groups of three on the main façade gave light to the third, fourth, and fifth floors. The sixth floor was opened by round headed windows. The geometry used in the design of the façade echoed the geometry of the mass. There was very little ornamentation on the exterior. Pilasters and corner turrets extended beyond the balustrade above a decorative cornice. The main entrance was a large round arched opening. In 1971 the building was razed.

Much the same description given to the Yates Hotel also fits the Dey Brothers Store, a flat-roofed, six-story block that was erected on the southeast corner of South Salina and East Jefferson Streets in Syracuse in 1893. Here again contemporary sources paid special attention to the novel equipment that had been installed in the building. The store was steam heated; it had electric light, elevators, an automatic sprinkler system and, above all, a

telephone system connected various parts of the building. Although the building still stands, there is not much left of the old store after a complete renovation in the 1960s.

50. **DEY BROTHERS DRY GOODS STORE (1893), South Salina and East Jefferson Streets, Syracuse, New York.** Altered. *Photo courtesy of Onondaga County Public Library.*

BEAUX-ARTS

In Syracuse Russell's Central High School (1901–1903) (plate 51) and the Fourth Onondaga County Courthouse (1904–1907) (plates 52–56) exemplify the Beaux-arts idea that public buildings should be executed in the grand monumental tradition of classical design.

In 1900 Russell submitted plans for a new high school to replace the old one which had become a health hazard. Apparently the separation of rooms for recitation and study purposes was the newest trend in school construction, and Russell was quick to embody it in the plans for Central High School. The building had the symmetrical Beaux-arts plan with a large assembly hall on the first floor as the core of the building. Study, class, and recitation rooms were symmetrically arranged around it.

The three-story brick structure facing Billings Park was to accommodate fifteen hundred students, and it was of slow-burning rather than fireproof construction. Iron stairways were used with wrought iron and wood balustrades. Metal and concrete were placed under the wood floor system, which was supported by iron columns. The main façade fronting Warren Street shows a three-part division with the central block emphasized by paired Ionic columns, which start on the second floor level and support an ornamented pediment. The entrance—for teachers and visitors—the pediment, and the cornices are richly decorated with classical ornamentation. Students used

51. Central High School (1901–1903), South Warren and Adams Streets, Syracuse, New York. *Photo courtesy of Onondaga Historical Association.*

the side entrance on East Adams Street. "Archimedes Russell's genius has created this magnificent building," reported the *Post-Standard* on January 30, 1903. In 1975 the building was abandoned and turned back to the city for disposition.

In 1902 Archimedes Russell was chosen to draw plans for the Fourth Onondaga County Courthouse. The new building included the latest in mechanical contrivances. It was steam heated and equipped with a "novel" vacuum sweeping system, the latest system of wiring (all wires for lighting and telephones were concealed in ducts), and five hydraulic elevators.

After several delays in construction the courthouse was finally dedicated in December 1906, and occupied soon after. Probably thinking of the debacle that was connected with the building of the State Capitol in Albany (1867–94), Syracusans were more than happy that this "great public structure was built without scandal or graft," as the Syracuse *Journal* noted on December 29, 1906. The heavy steel beam frame is clad in Indiana buff limestone. According to the *Post-Standard* of February 10, 1904, limestone was chosen for economic reasons. It could be sawed and worked by machinery without handwork, which would make it less expensive than the granite used in the Albany Capitol. Gray granite was used for bases, quoins, steps, and platforms. The symmetrical building is modeled after Italian Renaissance prototypes. It is crowned by a ribbed dome surmounted by a cupola and is anchored on its corners by four smaller domed towers. Giant composite columns carry the entablature and emphasize the main section.

Russell used sculpted wreaths in the frieze to accentuate each column and pilaster on the front façade (plate 53). The break between the first and the second levels is indicated by a stringcourse of classical detailing. The larger windows of the second story are round headed rather than trabeated, as are all the other windows except those in the dome and in the towers. The

52. FOURTH ONONDAGA COUNTY COURTHOUSE (1904–1907), Montgomery, State, and Jefferson Streets, Syracuse, New York.

53. FOURTH ONONDAGA COUNTY COURTHOUSE, Elevation of Third and Fourth Floors.

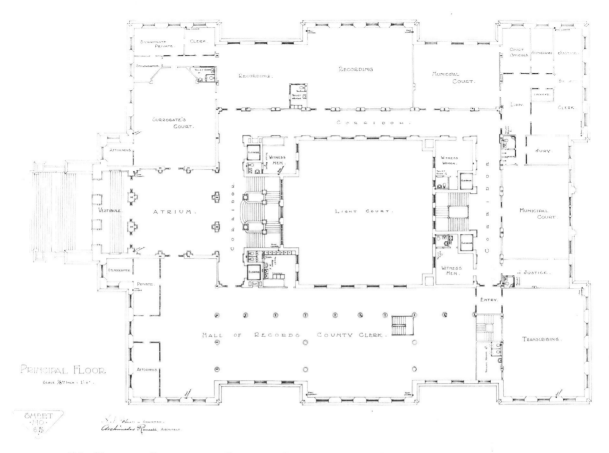

54. FOURTH ONONDAGA COUNTY COURTHOUSE, Plan. *Courtesy of Onondaga County Clerk's Office.*

arches springing from finely etched imposts are held by heavy keystones. The giant pilasters that unify the second and third stories are supported by a rusticated ground floor. The side façades are less ornamented. A classically detailed cornice with a balustrade terminates the third story.

The floor plan is similar to that of Central High School (plate 54). In each building a large core—the assembly hall in Central High School, the open light court in the courthouse—is encircled by a corridor from which the various other rooms can be reached.

The local firm of E. M. Allewelt & Brothers was given the interior decorating contract and, according to press reports, the public seemed to be more than pleased. The main lobby on the first floor, which was officially called the atrium, has marble columns and marble floors (plate 55). It is finished in dull gold and blues and has an ornate ceiling in plaster and metal. The walls are decorated with four murals of legendary as well as historical episodes from the area which is now Onondaga County. "The Death of Minnehaha," "The Ascension of Hiawatha," "The Discovery of Salt by Pere Le Moyne," and "Asa Danforth, Pioneer" were painted on canvas and cemented to the wall above the wainscoting. The artist was William De. L. Dodge of New York, who charged $4,000 for the paintings.

The fact that these paintings depict local history was indicative of a new development in mural painting. Painters and sculptors worked together with architects to represent the unity of the arts, the spirit of an American renaissance.

The second floor houses the municipal court (plate 56). The foyer is adorned with a floor of Tennessee marble arranged in a rug pattern, a decorative molded ceiling, and on the stair landing three murals symbolizing law and justice, painted by Gustav Gutgemon, who at the time taught painting at the Pratt Institute in New York. Marble pillars support the floor

55. FOURTH ONONDAGA COUNTY COURTHOUSE, Lobby Ceiling.

56. FOURTH ONONDAGA COUNTY COURTHOUSE, Courtroom.

above. Marble wainscoting eight feet high is found in all corridors. A Palladian motif was used in the entrance to the courtrooms. The doors are filled with leaded glass, as are those in the entrance to the surrogate court below. The leaded glass windows are framed with mahogany. In each suite a different wood is used. The woodwork behind the judges' benches in the courtrooms is elaborately carved.

In the 1950s changes in the courthouse were proposed, but the public protested. In 1959 the building was sandblasted, and a portion of the third floor of the courthouse was remodeled by King & King of Syracuse. Melvin King had been actively involved in the courthouse's original design. On the strength of its success Russell had made him a partner in the firm.

The Carnegie Public Library in Canastota (1901) (plate 57), and the First Universalist Church in Syracuse (1905) (plate 58), are also Russell interpretations of the Beaux-arts style.

57. **CARNEGIE PUBLIC LIBRARY (1901), Main and Center Streets, Canastota, New York.** This two-story brick building has a rectangular plan with a projecting center section. Neoclassical pilasters articulate the center section and the corners of the structure. Trabeated windows, rhythmically placed, light the interior. The pediment is emphasized by its size, a wreathlike ornamentation, and an egg and dart molding. The building served as prototype for a jail and powerhouse which Russell built four years later in Syracuse. *Photo courtesy of Canastota Public Library.*

58. First Universalist Church (1905), South Warren and East Adams Streets, Syracuse, New York. Demolished. The church, officially named Betts Memorial Universalist Church, was built of red brick in Neoclassical design. Dentils ornamented the pediments and cornices, arched openings were cut into the walls, and a small polygonal dome was placed in the center of the building. *Photo courtesy of Onondaga Historical Association.*

MISSION

Popular during the end of the nineteenth and the beginning of the twentieth centuries, Mission style is characterized by arches, tiles, low-pitched roofs, simplicity of form, and a general lack of surface decoration. In 1904 Mission style was discussed in *The Craftsman*, a journal edited and published by Gustav Stickley in Syracuse. In 1915 at the Panama-California Exposition celebrating the opening of the Panama Canal, visitors admired buildings designed in the Spanish Colonial Revival style which was only slightly different from Mission style.

Syracuse prided itself on having a fine example of Mission style church architecture (plate 59). The children of German immigrants, weary of having to listen to church services held in German, had organized the English Lutheran Church in 1879. The firm of Russell and King received the commission for the church building, which was ready for its first service in June 1911.

Ohio gray sandstone "tooled and dressed" was used for the structure, which was roofed with red tile. Fine stained glass windows in green and amber

59. FIRST ENGLISH LUTHERAN CHURCH (1910–11), 507 James Street, Syracuse, New York. Altered.

shades, in blue, purple, and yellow, were special features mentioned in the local press. The plan consists of a rectangular sanctuary with Sunday school rooms in the rear. The narthex is articulated by a large bell tower in the center and flanked by two smaller ones. All three towers are capped with pyramidal tile roofs. The main entrance, centrally placed in the large bell tower, has two doorways with leaded etched panes of glass. The roof of the main entrance and the side entrances in the smaller towers are supported by stone piers terminated by small curvilinear gables. The window openings are set flush into the smooth walls, yet there is more projecting ornamentation on the exterior than usual in the Mission style. This ornamentation is shown by the projecting piers on the east and west facades, the carved stone dentils in the large tower, the carved frieze above the main entrance, and the label molding above the narthex window. The wooden brackets of the entrance and tower roofs are similar to those used in Stick style buildings. The grillwork in the large bell tower is also similar to Stick style detailing.

As in the Prairie style houses of this time, there is great concern for geometric clarity, which is apparent in the organization of the windows, the grill work of the tower, the carved stone ornamentation, the articulation of the façades, and in the interior ceiling, which is divided into squares.

The crispness of the articulation as well as the emphasis on geometric clarity in the structure are quite different from the florid ornamentation and curved shapes more usual in Russell's work. Because of impaired health before his death in 1915, Russell may have relegated a large part of the office work to his partner Melvin King, and it is likely that King was also responsible for many of the designs during these later years. Although interior changes and additions have been made since its dedication in the fall of 1911, the First English Lutheran Church still stands on James and Townsend Streets in Syracuse.

SELECTED OTHER COMMISSIONS

1868   Zion Evangelical Lutheran Church, Butternut Street and Prospect Avenue, Syracuse, New York.

1870   *Sibley Hall, Cornell University, Ithaca, New York.
Independent Church, 457 South Salina Street, Syracuse, New York.
Auburn Theological Seminary Library, Seminary Street, Auburn, New York.
*Presbyterian Church, Clyde, New York.

1871   Fayetteville Baptist Church, East Genesee Street, Fayetteville, New York.
*West Genesee Street Methodist Church, 1700 West Genesee Street, Syracuse, New York.
*First Presbyterian Church, Seneca Falls, New York.

1872   *Cazenovia Methodist Church, Southwest corner of Seminary and Linklaen Streets, Cazenovia, New York.
*First Presbyterian Church, Waterville, New York.

*Extant

This list was selected from Archimedes Russell's account books now in the Syracuse University Archives and based on documented size of commission fee and/or historical importance.

1884   The Alhambra, Southwest corner of Pearl and James Streets, New York.
            Cortland House, Main and Groton Streets, Cortland, New York.
            The Greyhound Building, Northwest corner of James and Warren Streets,
                Syracuse, New York.

1886   *Furman Street Methodist Church, 104 Furman Street, Syracuse, New York.
            W. S. Peck Warehouse, West Water Street, Syracuse, New York.

1887   Second National Bank, Oswego, New York.

1888   *St. Joseph's Church (now the VFW Hall), Lafayette, New York.
            *H. B. Clark Residence, 7616 North Jefferson Street, Pulaski, New York.
            *St. Patrick's Church, Otisco, New York.
            Jacob Amos Residence, West Genesee Street, Syracuse, New York.

1889   House of Providence, Syracuse, New York (Town of Geddes).

1890   *George D. Whedon Residence, 672 West Onondaga Street, Syracuse,
                New York.
            *Assumption Church School Buildings, 812 North Salina (reconstructed) and
                1115 North Townsend Streets, Syracuse, New York.
            Grand Theater & Opera House, East Fayette Street, Syracuse, New York.
            *James A. Deveraux Building, Oneida, New York.
            *Remington Memorial Chapel (Methodist Church), Ilion, New York.

1891   *Francis Baumer Candle Factory, North Alvord Street, Syracuse, New York.
            Christian Cook Block, East Washington Street, Syracuse, New York.
            Thousand Islands Park Association Hotel (exact location unknown).

1892   Sacred Heart Church, Southest corner of Park Avenue and West Genesee Street, Syracuse, New York.

        *Church of the Immaculate Conception, Pompey, New York.

        *St. Agnes Church, 700 Kossuth Street, Utica, New York.

        *Canajoharie Academy, Cliff and Otsego Streets, Canajoharie, New York.

        *Masonic Lodge #415 F. & A.M., 7582 Broad Street, Pulaski, New York.

1894   *Reformed Church (chapel at rear of Church) (listed on National Register of Historic Places), 405 North Main Street, Herkimer, New York.

        St. Vincent de Paul Orphanage, Madison Street and Columbus Circle, Syracuse, New York.

1895   *F. W. Gridley Residence, 749 West Onondaga Street, Syracuse, New York.

1886   Edward Joy Residence, West Genesee Street, Syracuse, New York.

        *St. Joseph's Hospital (rehabilitated for nurses dormitory), Prospect Avenue, Syracuse, New York.

1898   Onondaga Pottery Factory Buildings (now Syracuse China), West Fayette Street, Syracuse, New York.

        *Little Falls High School (now the grade school), Little Falls, New York.

1899   *Pass & Seymour Factory, Milton and Boyd Avenues, Solvay, New York.

1900   Herriman Flats, West Onondaga Street, Syracuse, New York.

        *C. W. Snow Residence, University Avenue and Madison Street, Syracuse, New York.

1901   *German Evangelical Friedens Church (much altered), 1501 Lodi Street, Syracuse, New York.

        Isaac Rosenbloom Residence, East Genesee Street, Syracuse, New York.

1902   *Phillips Free Library, 27 South Main Street, Homer, New York.

1903   *Cathedral of the Immaculate Conception (towers only), Columbus Circle and Jefferson Street, Syracuse, New York.

1905   *C. V. Kellogg Residence, Albany and Willow Streets, Cazenovia, New York.

1906   Academy of Holy Names (dormitory, music hall, and gymnasium buildings), Rome, New York.
        *Cathedral of the Immaculate Conception (sanctuary, partially altered in 1950s), Columbus Circle and Jefferson Street, Syracuse, New York.

1908   *House of Providence, 1654 West Onondaga Street, Syracuse, New York.

1909   *Seth D. Baker Residence, Walnut Avenue and Adams Street, Syracuse, New York.

1910   St. Mary's of the Lake Church, Skaneateles, New York.
        *Fire Station and Jail, Jordan, New York.

SUGGESTED READING

Benson, John Bradley. "Archimedes Russell (1840–1915), Architect of Syracuse; His Life and Works." Master's thesis, Syracuse University, 1979.

Blumenson, John H. G. *Identifying American Architecture.* Nashville: American Association for State and Local History, 1977.

Burchard, John, and Bush-Brown, Albert. *The Architecture of America: A Social and Cultural History.* Boston: Little, Brown, 1966.

Downing, A. J. *The Architecture of Country Houses.* Reprint. New York: Dover, 1969.

Eastlake, Charles L. *Hints on Household Taste in Furniture, Upholstery and Other Details.* Reprint. New York: Dover, 1969.

Girouard, Mark. *Sweetness and Light, the Queen Anne Movement 1860 – 1900.* Oxford: Claredon Press, 1977.

Hardin, Evamaria. "The Architectural Legacy of Archimedes Russell." Master's thesis, Syracuse University, 1979.

Hitchcock, Henry-Russell. *The Architecture of H. H. Richardson and His Times.* Cambridge, Mass.: MIT Press, 1975.

Jordy, William H. *American Ideals and their Architects.* Progressive and Academic Ideals at the Turn of the Twentieth Century, vol. 3. Garden City, N.Y.: Anchor Press/Doubleday, 1976.

Pierson, William H. *American Buildings and their Architects.* The Colonial and Neoclassical Styles, vol. 1. Garden City, N.Y.: Anchor Press/Doubleday, 1976.

Schuyler, Montgomery. *American Architecture and Other Writings,* edited by William H. Jordy and Ralph Coe. New York: Atheneum, 1964.

Scully, Vincent J. *The Shingle Style and the Stick Style: Architectural Theory and Design from Downing to the Origins of Wright.* New Haven: Yale University Press, 1977.

Stanton, Phoebe B. *Gothic Revival and American Church Architecture: An Episode in Taste, 1840 – 1856.* Baltimore: Johns Hopkins University Press, 1968.

Whiffin, Marcus. *American Architecture since 1780: A Guide to the Styles.* Cambridge, Mass.: MIT Press, 1977.